CW01668237

WOMEN AND LEADERSHIP IN IGBOLAND

OMOKU, IME CHI AND OMUGWO INSTITUTIONS

T. AKACHI EZEIGBO

Women and Leadership In Igboland
Omoku, Ime Chi and Omugwo Institutions

ISBN: 978-978-987-871-0

Published in Nigeria by:
Purple Shelves Publishers
Plot 1/3 Sam Ulaikere Crescent,
Royal Palmwill Estate,
Badore Town, Ajah, Lekki,
Lagos State
info@purpleshelves.com
www.purpleshelves.com
0816 924 1665

Credits:
(The Purple Shelves Team)
Editing: Amarachukwu Chimeka
Design: Charles Popson

DEDICATION

To my Mother,
Christiana Ukadinma Adimora
(1927-2015)

PREFACE

One of the issues trending in scholarship today is "decolonisation of knowledge". How can knowledge be decolonised in tertiary institutions to make allowances for an integrative and inclusive future that makes for social justice? In the so-called global world, whose knowledge counts? Whose knowledge matters? Whose knowledge is being exposed or privileged and whose knowledge is being undervalued? Between 19th and 24th October 2020, the School of Oriental and African Studies of the University of London had a week-long event tagged Virtual SOAS Festival of Ideas where issues of decolonising knowledge in tertiary institutions and the media were addressed. In a world in which many people describe themselves as both local and global individuals, it is important to ensure that knowledge of the local and the global are privileged so that more spaces can be opened in the dissemination of knowledge of various types for the purpose of solving both local and global problems as well as exposing useful and empowering ideas from even the remotest parts of the world for the benefit of everyone.

I am of the opinion that as we go global, we must not forget to remain local in order to propagate good ideas from the local landscape that will benefit us and the future generation. The renowned novelist and essayist, Chinua Achebe, said that to be universal is to be truly local. As a local and global Nigerian, I would like to raise the consciousness of my people to appreciate our culture, especially positive aspects of it that existed in the past but are now fading from our collective memory – for the purpose of social and cultural redirection. We need to claim the knowledge of the present as well as reclaim the knowledge of the past to be able to align ourselves properly in the pursuit of the knowledge of the future. When we reclaim the knowledge of the past, we would understand ourselves better and be able to take from it what is relevant to our lives in the 21st century and thereafter apply it to solve today's challenges.

One of the greatest things that shaped my life was my dual upbringing in the rural area and in the city during the years I was growing up in the then Eastern Region of Nigeria. Though my parents were practising Christians, they were conscious of the tradition and culture of their people and did all they could to preserve them and pass what they considered positive and relevant to their children. I am a beneficiary of this heritage. The formative years of my life were spent in the rural areas of Ekwulobia and Uga and later in the city of Port Harcourt. The experiences I garnered during these remarkable years of my life worked together to prepare me for the succeeding years of my life and moulded me to become what I am today. With the eyes of a child I observed women whose lifestyles and activities shaped my consciousness of what a woman should be and aspire to be – honest, decent, economically independent, supportive and caring. Of course, my mother, Christiana Ukadinma Adimora, was in the forefront of leading these remarkable bevy of hardworking, strong, and courageous women. Their leadership capabilities in the home and public spaces were phenomenal and they managed their affairs in the various communal and religious groups they belonged, especially in the Umuada (Association of Daughters) and Alutaradi (Association of Wives).

I remember with nostalgia the excitement I felt as a child when any of these two associations came out in large numbers to protest against an injustice or support a good cause. It was great. They would march forward with strength and determination to make their voices heard and their desires known. These early impressions of women's strengths and abilities must have laid the solid foundation for my research into women's condition, especially as foregrounded in the writing of not only Nigerian but also African women writers. My research in this direction necessitated my studying and analysing the works of female novelists, including Flora Nwapa, Buchi Emecheta, Bessie Head, Ama Ata Aidoo, Rebecca Njau, Ifeoma Okoye, Zaynab Alkali, Amma Darko, Yvonne Vera, Nawal El Saadawi, and younger writers, including Chimamanda Ngozi Adichie, Chika Unigwe, Promise Ogochukwu, Sefi Atta, Lola Shoneyin, NoViolet Bulawayo, Kaine Agary, Unoma Azuah, Chibundu Onuzo and many more. However, I have not limited myself to studying only women in modern African literature. I have devoted a reasonable amount of my research efforts to the lives of women of the past in Igbo culture in order to make their experiences known to modern women for the purpose of individual and societal reorientation, redirection and re-education. There is a lot modern women can learn from the women of the past.

In recent years I am appalled by the worsening condition of women in the Nigerian society and the unspeakable increase in the number of women subjugated and raped and the cases constantly reported in the electronic, print and social media. The reports on rape have become a daily occurrence in newspapers and on television and seem to have worsened in 2020 since the coronavirus pandemic surfaced. Gender-based violence is on the increase. It appears that the emancipation of women and the recognition of their rights as "human rights" have retrogressed and that the hope of liberating women from all forms of patriarchal oppression is lost.

One way to counter women's loss of dignity and halt the abuse of women's rights is to put in place proper legislations that would not only protect women but also safeguard their lives and interests. Another way which I promote by publishing this research is to make known the leadership roles women of the past played in their community that enabled them not only to protect themselves and their families but also assert their humanity and their rights to respect and independence. This monograph, *Women and Leadership in Igboland Omoku, Ime Chi and Omugwo Institutions,* aims to empower women with the knowledge that, like their foremothers, they have a right to hold leadership positions not only in the home but also in the workplace and public space. An understanding of women's leadership position in the home ought to enable society appreciate the fact that issues such as domestic violence, rape, gender oppression, or domination must not be tolerated. Women are generally indispensable in society, particularly in the home. Therefore, their rights and well-being must be safeguarded at all times by society and by themselves.

T. Akachi Ezeigbo
Lagos, 2020.

ABSTRACT

Contrary to Basden's opinion that the condition of Igbo women – in the early twentieth century when he lived among Ndi Igbo – was pitiable and totally subjugated, the truth is that Igbo women enjoyed a measure of independence, especially in the areas of taking charge of their own affairs and empowering themselves, economically. This fact could be seen in the way they controlled their socio-political organisations such as the Umuada and the Alutaradi. In this study I examine women's leadership roles in another sphere of influence under women's control: Omoku, Ime Chi and Omugwo institutions. I argue that there were a variety of leadership opportunities open to Igbo women in the past – some of them still exist today and will continue to exist in the years to come – through which they exerted and can still exert their influence to ensure the well-being of their families and communities.

INTRODUCTION

Basden's opinion that the condition of Igbo women – in the early twentieth century when he lived among Ndi Igbo – was pitiable and totally subjugated is palpably contestable when one carefully studies the experience of women in various communities in different parts of Igboland, particularly in the old Aguata Local Government Area where this researcher comes from[1] and where Basden largely carried out his missionary work. He claimed that "Women have but few rights in any circumstance and can only hold such property as their lords permit. There is no grumbling against their lot; they accept the situation as their grandmothers did before them and, taking affairs philosophically, they manage to live fairly contentedly," (1921: 88). Though a highly effective and motivational missionary of the Church Missionary Society (CMS), Basden,

...demonstrates a lack of knowledge of the socio-political system of power distribution and the concept of role differentiation in terms of gender and sex among the Igbo in the society of that time. He fails to appreciate the different political and social systems and mechanisms through which women exercised power and managed their own affairs among the Igbo of old Onitsha Province, particularly Aguata LGA – the area in which he lived and worked. His book was published in 1921 and barely eight years later, the famous *Aba Women's War* was "waged", between 1929 and 1931, covering an area of the old Owerri Province. Again Igbo women demonstrated that whenever necessary, they could rise up in defence of their tradition and right not to be taxed as women. In Uga, the area of Igboland where I come from, women had rights and asserted themselves in the patriarchy by controlling their own affairs, especially through the powerful association of daughters and association of wives of the land known as Umuada and Alutaradi respectively. Before the colonial incursion and the subjugation of Uga community under British colonial administration in the late 19th century, these women groups "controlled their own affairs, defended their rights, enforced decisions unanimously taken, and generally maintained political influence in the patriarchy that was patterned to marginalise them" (Ezeigbo,

Gender Issues in Nigeria: 1996, 68).

Umuada also exercised power in the leadership cadre and policy-making body called Obuofo through their representatives called Oluada – Voice of Women or Spokesperson for women. This phenomenon is beautifully illustrated in my historical novel, *The Last of the Strong Ones* (1996).

The work done by some scholars[2], especially women anthropologists and historians mostly in the second half of the twentieth century have gone a long way to document the activities and roles women played in pre-colonial and colonial periods of Igbo history. In these well-researched papers, the scholars tried to show that Igbo women were able to take charge of their affairs in socio-political and economic issues and fairly maintained a measure of independence from their men as well as occasionally resisted any tyrannical acts meted out to them by the patriarchal society. Amadiume, for example, has this to say about Igbo women's determination to demand justice when necessary: "At the worst, if lineage men proved stubborn, wives went on strike, in which case they would refuse to cook for or have sexual intercourse with their husbands..." (65).

Another good illustration of this resistance and power to act independently is seen when groups of women (wives, especially) "sit" on their men whenever they felt unjustly treated as examined in Judith van Allen's essay "Sitting on a Man: Colonialism and the Lost Political Institution of Igbo Women" (1972: 165-181). The wielding of this political power to "sit" on men is graphically explored in Akachi Adimora-Ezeigbo's historical novel *The Last of the Strong Ones* (1996) Moreover, Leith-Ross documents in her remarkable book, *African Women* (1939: 337), the leadership abilities and fiercely independent spirit of Igbo women. She describes Igbo women as "a rare and invaluable force, thousands upon thousands of ambitious, go-ahead, courageous, self-reliant, hardworking, independent women," and stresses their "startling energy, their power of organisation and leadership."

The leadership roles played by women in Igbo culture are yet to be widely researched so that this aspect of women's contribution to the history and development of Igboland in general and Igbo communities in particular would be properly documented for the benefit of Ndi Igbo, especially the youths and those who aspire to play leadership roles now and in the future. Women's contribution to Igbo leadership covers a multitude of spheres – the economy, politics, culture, technology, religion, etc.

When I was growing up, I was privileged to live in Ekwulobia and Uga towns in the Aguata Local Government Area of Anambra State. I also traversed other towns like Aguluezechukwu, Oko, Nanka, Isuofia, Igbo Ukwu, Amesi, Nkpologwu, Achina, Akpo, Umuchu, etc. also in the same local government, which was then known as Aguata County Council. My father rose from the ranks to the position of District Officer (DO) in the county council, and this provided a conducive environment for me to get to know the culture and customs of these towns. My mother was a strong influence on the women of the area and played an important role in empowering them as she related with some of them individually and in some of their organisations as the wife of the District Officer. It is interesting to mention here that it was my mother that introduced many of the women in the area to planting *ugu* and using this very important vegetable in cooking various dishes. She was also a famous baker and seamstress. It was, therefore, relatively easy for me to get to know the activities of the women of the area and learn so much about women's culture in the county council area in the course of observing some of the religious – traditional and Christian – worships and festival, visiting markets, fetching water from rivers or streams, and participating in farm work. Many years later, I decided to research into some of the women's institutions in these places, especially in Uga, my hometown. The result of these research efforts are my creative writing (especially in the Umuga trilogy, *The Last of the Strong Ones*, *House of Symbols* and *Children of the Eagle*), my academic work and my performance of celebratory dirges.

An aspect of my research in women's roles in Igboland that I find most satisfying is the one dealing with leadership. In this study, I examine women's leadership roles in the home – a special sphere of influence largely under women's control. In the traditional past, it was in the home that women, especially mothers, exercised their power to observe and celebrate the Omoku, Ime Chi and Omugwo rituals. The Omugwo institution existed and still exists all over Igboland, while the Omoku and Ime Chi (now extinct) flourished in the Aguata area of Anambra State, particularly in Uga Town, strategically located at the boundaries of Anambra and Imo States, in the pre-colonial and colonial periods, and was abolished when Christianity became fully established in the area.

In this study, I discuss the content and form as well as the functions of these three institutions based on the interviews I conducted with three elderly matriarchs from my town, Uga, where these institutions held sway in the past and where the Omugwo ritual, the only surviving one among the three, is still practised as it is in other Igbo communities in and outside Nigeria[3]. I also argue in this study that there were a variety of leadership opportunities open to Igbo women in the past that still exist today and will continue to exist in the years to come, through which they exerted and can still exert their influence to ensure the well-being of their families and communities. In the next section, I define, analyse and discuss the function of each in the Igbo society. Omoku and Ime Chi rituals have become extinct, but Omugwo is still very much alive and practised extensively wherever Igbo people settle.

CONTENT AND FORM OF OMOKU, IME CHI AND OMUGWO INSTITUTIONS

OMOKU

Omoku can be regarded as a domestic or family festival, for it is observed by every mature married woman who has a daughter. It is a celebration of motherhood and fertility; it reminds a woman of the privilege of being a mother who has perpetuated herself through procreation and by giving birth to a female child or children[4]. During Omoku celebration, a mother performs the ritual with her female child(ren) or invites her daughter(s) home if she is married to celebrate the occasion with her. The daughter(s) could visit with her young children if she has children. This means that only a woman of a mature age celebrates Omoku.

On the day of the ceremony, the celebrating mother wakes up early to prepare a special sauce made with snails – a delicacy among Uga people. Her daughter or daughters will assist her if she wishes. Then, she pounds some foofoo, which will be eaten with the sauce. The ritual, which has a spiritual undertone, requires the mother to place four small balls of foofoo dipped generously in the sauce and put on a wooden tray placed on the floor of her room. Her daughter(s) stoops low and with her mouth (not her hand) picks up the small balls of foofoo and eats them. She also eats four snails from the same tray by picking them up with her mouth. Only female children are allowed to eat this food. The ritual symbolises an act of solidarity between mother and daughter. It also shows the power and influence the mother has over her daughter, and places her in an important position to exercise her limited leadership role in the home. It allows for intimacy between them and enables them to re-enact the nurturing gesture of motherhood and the close affinity between Igbo women and their daughters, especially their first daughters[5].

After the performance of this ritual, feasting commences, and the mother serves her husband and male children the food she has prepared for the celebration. Afterwards, she retires to a quiet place and has a heart-to-heart discussion with her daughter(s) – what some people call "women talk".

IME CHI

Ime Chi is a special act of worship allowed every woman from Uga once a year to show gratitude to her personal god or what can be best described in Christian terminology as her Guardian Angel. As in Omoku ritual, the woman celebrates the day by cooking a good meal for her family. But the day begins by her sacrificially killing a chicken and cooking the meal at a special point in the compound, close to an odoala tree[6] which she has dedicated to her Chi. An ogirisi (umune) tree can also serve the same purpose as odoala; it is another sacred or revered plant used by Ndi Igbo to perform rituals. Though the woman alone performs the ritual, the whole family, including her husband, will eat the meal she has prepared in celebration of her Chi. Some of the special foods prepared are utara ede or une ojii, to be served with oha or bitterleaf soup. This is a very important occasion for the woman. All eyes are on her; she is the focus of attention in the family and her role as a mother, wife, and an individual are acknowledged and celebrated by her loved ones, including her husband and her children. Indeed, the entire household honours her. Her spiritual well-being is thus acknowledged and endorsed by her husband and children and she has the unique opportunity and privilege to commune with her Chi – personal god or guardian spirit – as demonstrated in the sacrifice she makes to her Chi.

OMUGWO

The third women-centred institution discussed in this paper is Omugwo, the only one among the three that survived colonisation, Christianisation, modernity and globalisation. Omugwo is still practised in its near-pure form by Ndi Igbo though modernisation and globalisation may have brought about some modifications in the performance. When a woman gives birth, her mother is immediately invited to look after her, irrespective of whether it is her first child or not. This means that a woman continues to enjoy Omugwo each time she gives birth to a baby[7]. Igbo women have taken the practice of Omugwo even beyond the confines of Igboland and Nigeria. It has become a global phenomenon as Igbo women in the diaspora routinely invite their mothers to the global North (Europe and North America) when they have babies to perform Omugwo and help them take care of the babies and relieve them of the stress encountered in living in the West as people of colour with the attendant racism and other disadvantages African immigrants suffer in these lands. If their mothers are not available or are late, the women invite their aunts or elder sisters.

According to Obiabaka, when coming, the mother

> ... prepared her mind to stay as long as possible, until the woman was able to help herself with domestic duties. While coming, the mother or relation of the woman brought along with her assorted spices, dried fish and dried meat with which she would cook for the woman. On the eight day the child was sent to a native midwife for circumcision... At the end of the 'Omugwo', the mother of the woman would receive plenty of presents from the son-in-law. The son-in-law would buy some clothing, and edible presents which his mother-in-law would take to her house. In some cases,

> presents like salt or soaps were included for the women married in the same kindred with her. (109-110)

A woman can stay for three or four months for Omugwo. Some stay for six months or more. It depends on her convenience or sometimes the family's. While performing this ritual, she is responsible for bathing the new baby, cooking nourishing food for her daughter and taking care of her, and giving her emotional support and helping her daughter to run her home while she recuperates from the stress of childbirth and the regular post-natal physical and psychological trauma that can cause depression for some women, especially if left on their own.

WOMEN'S LEADERSHIP ROLES IN THE HOME FRONT: THE EXAMPLES OF OMOKU, IME CHI AND OMUGWO

Leadership has been described as influence. If leaders influence people and have the skills to command people's respect, then women invariably attain this status in the home, where they occupy an important position. This is particularly the case in Igbo culture where women, specifically mothers, are respected and revered. The Yoruba say, "Mother is gold," but Ndi Igbo say, "Mother is supreme." It is somewhat paradoxical that women are often subjugated and marginalised in Igbo patriarchy but are also highly regarded as daughters in the lineage and as mothers in the family. Consequently, though women may not play prominent political or religious[8] roles in many parts of Igboland, they wield a reasonable amount of power in the home where their leadership qualities shine most luminously.

The ritual performance of Ime Chi or Omoku places much responsibility on the mother who observes it. Ime Chi allows her to be the master of her own destiny and to take responsibility of her spiritual welfare and that of her children by sacrificing to her Chi and leading her family to participate in the celebration. She guides them through the process of prioritising worship, togetherness, unity and peace. The same spirit is maintained in Omoku. In performing the ritual, the woman exercises some power over her children, especially her daughters. It is a time she is in close communion with her daughters and can give them instruction and listen to them and give valuable advice to then, especially her married daughter(s). This is particularly the case with Omoku. The period of the celebration allows her to relate closely to them to find out if they have challenges in their marital home so she can counsel them. Daughters "return home" briefly to draw strength from their mothers and "suck her breasts again", as Ndi Igbo put it.

A woman's leadership role in the home during the Omoku celebration is best demonstrated by a scene from my novel *The Last of the Strong Ones* where the widow, Onyekozuru, is tutored and effectively counselled by her mother. Onyekozuru fell in love with Obiatu, a single man who later met the fascinating Ejimnaka and married her, abandoning his lover, Onyekozuru. In an unhappy state, the widow arrived at her mother's for Omoku and was persuaded to bare her mind. Her mother gave her sound counsel. Onyekozuru reported that it was

> ...a story about the raven who wanted to exchange its beautiful and shiny black feathers for the white feathers of the egret. The raven went to the river and bathed itself for a long time, but its colour would not change. No matter how hard it tried, it could not achieve its desire. Rather, its beautiful black feathers looked dull and worn after all the repeated washing... She ended by saying that Obiatu was out of my reach. If I pined away forever, I would still not have him, for he would not leave his wife for me...
>
> For many days I thought about what my mother said. The parable

> of the raven began to make sense. I must not hunger after what I could not have or it would break my spirit and dry my bones. My mother had advised me to make friends with Ejimnaka... You know, that was exactly what I did. (51-52).

The novel tells us that for the rest of their lives, Onyekozuru and Ejimnaka become great friends and close allies in the community of Umuga. Omoku celebration brings mother and daughter together and enables the mother to redirect her daughter's life and lead her on the path to future happiness and greatness. This is leadership of the finest quality.

Such leadership influence is equally apparent in relation to the Omugwo institution. Though a mother has to travel[9] to her daughter's home to perform the Omugwo, her leadership skills are equally put into good use in her son-in-law's home. Her arrival cheers everyone up, for she will immediately take over the responsibility of taking care of the house and everyone, especially her daughter, the nursing mother, and her son-in-law. There is a general sigh of relief when she arrives. A great illustration of the wonder and beauty of Omugwo ritual cannot perhaps be found anywhere else than in a short story, "Grand Experience" published in an anthology titled *Wings of Dawn*. Exploring the experience of a first-time grandmother, the story highlights some of the responsibilities attached to the institution and what is expected of a woman who finds herself in this situation. The protagonist's ruminations are graphically conveyed in the following words:

> This new joy carries with it much responsibility. The omugwo ritual, which you're now performing for your daughter, is a whole lot of multifaceted adventure. You are beginning to learn to keep awake at night even when you don't want to. The baby wakes up many times and the tired mother needs your assistance as the experienced mother who must be forthright with advice, with instructions. The dos and don'ts of this grand period must be spelt out unequivocally. You must tell her when the baby

> is hot and when the cover cloth must be divested for the baby to feel comfortable. You must insist that the baby should be fed on demand. You should teach her to rub the baby's back after feeding until he belches. The young and inexperienced mother has a lot to learn from you... That's how it is. Much demand is made on your time and your body. On your emotions and your mind as well.
>
> The new mother needs rest; she needs help with the baby. Her mother, the grandmother satisfies this need and offers help easily and willingly (115-116, 119).

Omugwo performance gives a woman room to contribute to the well-being of her daughter and her household in a very unique and special way. She assists to welcome a baby into the world and helps in the nurturing of the little one in the first few months of their life. It is a tasking but rewarding responsibility which each mother prays and hopes to enjoy in her lifetime, many times with each of her female children.

CONCLUSION

From the foregoing, it is quite clear that a woman has special leadership roles to play in the Igbo world. The institutions of Ime Chi, Omoku and Omugwo showcase these responsibilities so graphically. That few people have written about women's activities in these spheres shows how women's leadership functions, roles and activities have been neglected and relegated to the background. More research needs to be made in these institutions and others where women played and still play important roles that contributed and still contribute to the welfare of Igbo families and communities.

Our discussions in the study show that Igbo women were and are involved in leadership by service and example. In each institution, women are shown to lead by serving people, especially their families. They are ready to sacrifice their time and lives and render quality service that endears them to their families, particularly their children. They can be referred to as "servant leaders",[10] which is regarded as the finest type of leadership. A classic example of this form of leadership was demonstrated by the Lord Jesus Christ, the good shepherd, ready to die for the sheep and willing to wash the feet of his disciples to show them what true service and humility means.

NOTES

1. See my article "Traditional Women's Institutions in Igbo Society: Implications for the Igbo Female Writer". *African Languages and Cultures* 3. 2 (1990): 149-165.

2. Two well-known examples are Ifi Amadiume, *Male Daughters, Female Husbands*. London: Zed Books Ltd, 1987 and Nina Emma Mba, *Nigerian Women Mobilized: Women's Political Activity in Southern Nigeria, 1900-1965*. Berkeley: University of California Press, 1982.

3. It is interesting that the Omugwo institution is practised wherever Igbo people live or settle. Many Igbo families living in other parts of Nigeria – outside the Igbo homeland in the South East of Nigeria and even in the diaspora – observe Omugwo. Many mothers travel to Europe and America, etc. to perform Omugwo for their daughters,

thereby keeping the ritual alive.

4. Though male children are valued more than female children among the Igbo, especially in the past, daughters are regarded as a source of wealth. Hence, female children are given names such as Aboego (Basket of money), Akunna (Father's wealth), Akuoma (Good/beautiful wealth), Nwakuabia (A bringer of wealth has come), etc.

5. It is almost always the case that a woman's first daughter (called Ada in Igbo language) is the closest to her. She is the one she relies on, confides in, and entrusts her affairs; she is the one most likely to take care of her and nurse her if she falls sick. This is why most Igbo women, especially in Uga, desire their first daughters to marry from their towns so that their daughters will be available whenever they require help or advice. First daughters have great influence in their natal homes.

6. Odoala is a shrub that grows well throughout the year and is symbolic of life and stability. It has healing properties and is also used to mark boundaries to protect family or communal land. It lives for a long time

and does not die easily unless deliberately destroyed or uprooted. It is an abomination when an aggrieved party or individual uproots it as a boundary marker in a land dispute without seeking the mediation of family or community. Odoala is resilient and has a white sap used to treat wounds.

7. If the mother of the nursing mother is no longer alive or is sick, an aunt or elder sister would be sent for.

8. In most parts of Igboland, especially in Aguata Local Government Area and Uga town (where specifically this research was carried out) women were not allowed to be priestesses of the numerous deities, not even of the female deities such as Idemmiri and Isigwu. These two powerful goddesses had priests who worshipped them.

9. Times are changing and Omugwo is being modified by many Igbo families. There are cases these days when the mother invites her daughter to her own home rather than travel to her daughter's to perform the ritual. This is particularly the case where the woman is working or is holding an important responsibility in government or

the private sector, which would not allow her move from her location to where her daughter lives with her family. In this way, the woman is able to continue with her work as well as take care of her daughter and grandchild.

10. The term "servant leader" is often used in Nigeria by politicians. For example, the then Governor of Niger State, Babangida Aliyu, described himself as a servant leader – specifically, Chief Servant of Niger State.

ACKNOWLEDGEMENTS

I am grateful to my sister-in-law, Madam Ijeaku Ezenwamiriaku (85 years old), Madam Ajunwa Onyelonu (85 Years old) and Madam Uloaku Ibeakanma (99 years old) who provided useful information on the three institutions particularly on the extinct Omoku and Ime Chi rituals. Without their help I could not have got the detailed information I needed to be able to discuss Omoku and Ime Chi rituals. I also thank Lantern Books, a division of Literamed Publications (Nig.) Limited, for the excerpt taken from *The Last of the Strong Ones.* I gratefully acknowledge British Council, Nigeria and Women Writers of Nigeria (WRITA), Lagos, for "Grand Experience", a short story first published in *Wings of Dawn, An Anthology of New Writing by Nigerian Women* edited by Akachi Adimora-Ezeigbo and Veronica Ugbomma Uzoigwe, Lagos: British Council, 2006.

WORKS CITED

Akam, Uche J. B. *The Mustard-Seed – Uga: An Ecclesial Cell in a Local Church*. Onitsha, 1987.

Allen, Judith van. "Sitting on a Man:" Colonialism and the Lost Political Institutions of Igbo Women. *Canadian Journal of African Studies / Revue Canadienne des Études Africaines*, vol. 6, no. 2, Special Issue (1972): 165-181.

Amadiume, Ifi. *Male Daughters, Female Husbands*. London: Zed Books Ltd, 1987.

Anaedobe, M. M. and Ezenwaka, Titus N. *A Short History of Uga*. Onitsha, 1982.

Basden, G. T. *Among the Ibos of Nigeria* (1921). Onitsha: University Publishing Company, 1983.

Ezeigbo, T. Akachi. "Traditional Women's Institutions in Igbo Society: Implications for the Igbo Female Writer". *African Languages and Culture*, vol. 3, no. 2, 149-65.

--------------. *Gender Issues in Nigeria A Feminine*

Perspective. Lagos: Vista Books, 1996.

Adimora-Ezeigbo, Akachi. *The Last of the Strong Ones*. Lagos: Vista Books, 1996. Ikeja, Lagos: Lantern Books, 2006.

---------------. *House of Symbols*. Lagos: Oracle Books, 2001. Lagos: Lantern Books, 2006.

---------------. *Children of the Eagle*. Lagos: Vista Books, 2003. Lagos: Lantern Books, 2005.

Adimora-Ezeigbo, Akachi and Uzoigwe, Veronica Ugbomma. (Eds). *Wings of Dawn, An Anthology of New Writing by Nigerian Women*. Lagos: Women Writers of Nigeria (WRITA) Lagos & British Council Nigeria, 2006.

Leith-Ross, S. *African Women*. London: Faber and Faber, 1939.

Mba, Nina Emma. *Nigerian Women Mobilized: Women's Political Activity in Southern Nigeria, 1900-1965*. Berkeley: University of California Press, 1982.

Obiabaka, Amamchukwu. *History of Uga*. Printed in Nigeria by Lumos Nigeria Ltd., 2013.

APPENDIX I

"GRAND EXPERIENCE"

Dear Zimela,

You wrote: "*You're coping fine, I hope?*"

I have asked myself this and other questions many times, in the past one month. I'm progressing to a stage of ineluctable self-definition. Who am I? What will become of me in twenty years, if I live that long? How many more times will *this* responsibility choose me? Does my new status require changing my lifestyle? One in this situation is expected to show a good example, you know, be a role model of a sort. I'm beginning to confront my personal ghost of yesteryears. Experience long had and forgotten is back to haunt and imprison me. I'm the mother-of-a-mother! A grand experience! Yes, it's that complicated and simple. On the twentieth day of the first month of the year, I experienced my own special Epiphany – bearing three gifts of love, peace, and faith, as I went to see my grandson.

"*You're coping fine, I hope*?" your mail queried. I sensed a paradox in your concern for my well-being and your joy regarding my new state – grandmother. You commented on my physique: so "*ungrandmotherly*". I think I know what you meant. In me there is obvious absence of a maternal look – that solid full-bodied presence, with a thick waistline, broad hips and a prominent backside. You concluded your mail by repeating your question: "*My friend, I do hope you are coping well with your new responsibility?*"

A million *naira* question!

Yes, I'm struggling on. In the midst of my daily activities, I steal a few minutes just to muse. Gone are those carefree days of my youthful years. Blissful and inviolate. Where is the sense of freedom I felt and embraced with passion then? It seems as though I'm living my life all over. Trouble is, the shine is gone from it all, and I do not have the energy that I once had. Sap-strung, the years have come and gone, sapping cherished zeal in some things that once seemed indispensable. Gone is the energy that aided me to stay up, hour after hour, reading the features of my babies like a book, which had to be studied to pass an important examination. My musings compelled me to explore my feelings more concretely. How else could one do this but by sublimating it in *poesy*? I sing a song of myself for myself, in these lines. I address me as *other.* By so doing I address you and others who have arrived at this state or will arrive in the course of their journey, on this planet. I have a self outside me, as it were. A second self whom I address at will, these days. Is this part of the dividend of my new status? Is it an affliction of grannies?

I say to myself: *You know life has changed. You knew it was bound to change. You knew it that day the stranger who became your son led her to the altar. Then, your being a granny was just a matter of time. But now you occupy the position. You attain full knowledge of the fact that you're older. Older, both experience wise and age wise. Since it happened, since your first grandchild arrived, you have gained immense knowledge of mothers and newborn babies – far more than you did since you first occupied the enviable, privileged status of a mother. In the early years of your marriage, the flush of your youth. Then you were involved firsthand; now you are semi-detached.*

This new joy carries with it much responsibility. The omugwo ritual, which you're now performing for your daughter, is a whole lot of multifaceted adventure. You are beginning to learn to keep awake at night even when you don't want to. The baby wakes up many times and the tired mother needs your assistance as the experienced mother who must be forthright with advice, with instructions. The dos and don'ts of this **grand** *period must be spelt out unequivocally. You must tell her when the baby is hot and when the cover cloth must be divested for the baby to feel comfortable. You must insist that the baby should be fed on demand. You should teach her to rub the baby's back after feeding until he belches. The young and inexperienced mother has a lot to learn from you.*

That's how it is. Much demand is made on your time and your body. On your emotions and your mind as well. You're baffled, intrigued and exhilarated by the things you see and hear:

Watching the little one's elfin face
Listening to the rhythm of baby language
Flowing from the newcomer's tremulous breath
Replaying the music of countless births
Of young souls visiting the world of darkness and light
Amid oceans of goodwill, oases of peace in arid zones of evil.

You admit you're enjoying this new experience. A grand(motherly)experience. You, too, are learning, just like the young mother. When last did you nurse a baby? Why, over twenty years ago. Can you imagine? Now you're a mother again, though a **grand** *one; you're close to a newborn child. Your friends and colleagues write to hail you as "the latest grandmother in town". Some say "the youngest-looking grandma ever." They heap encomium upon you. You relish the epicurean delight of their meaty comments:*

"Now you're a top grandmother as well as a top professional," a friend crooned. "I can't believe it, you look so young."

"Welcome to grandmotherhood," a colleague, who is a grandmother, enthused. "With your tranquil spirit, I'm sure you'll be a wonderful support to your daughter and her new baby."

[Me? Tranquil? I wonder.]

Another friend wrote: "Your daughter and grandson are blessed in having a wonderful caring mother and grandmother and I wish you strength in your task of nurturing them at the start of this new stage in their family."

"May the little boy grow up to be a splendid man!" prayed a close male colleague.

A male acquaintance I meet at social gatherings enthused: "I never imagined, from your looks that you have a married daughter."

You bathe in the clear spring of effusive solidarity. You feel flattered. You feel good. All the kind and complimentary words mellow your heart: you decide to do your best for your daughter and grandson. It's worth it, you tell yourself. You will give them quality time and care. There is a lot of work to do to get organized. Organized. That's the idea.

You are getting to know more about babies than when you had your own children. See how excited you feel just sitting and watching this little tot wriggling his legs and waving his arms. It's all a novelty to you over again. You even rehearse the lullabies you learnt long ago. You sing them to the little one when he cries. When he is about to sleep or when he wakes up and screams for food.

Sleep, my little one, sleep, my pretty one
Float on the starry stream
World of all loveliness, wonderful world
Filling your magical dreams

Sleep, sleep, float on the starry stream
World of wonders fill your dreams.

All this and more I say to myself. I derive great pleasure ruminating over these issues, singing lullabies and talking to myself. I'm a woman performing *omugwo* for my daughter. I'm only doing for her what my mother did for me, what her mother did for her. In short, what our foremothers did for their daughters. It's a tradition every mother followed and still follows.

However, I have come a long way, in a period of one month. That's putting it in the mildest term. Among my people, o*mugwo* requires a mother to move into her daughter's home whenever a baby arrives. (Do you, by any chance, have such a tradition among your people, the Zulu?). The new mother needs rest; she needs help with the baby. Her mother – the grandmother – satisfies this need and offers help easily and willingly. Her visit could last a month or extend to between two and six months. It won't be strange if it stretches to a year. A recent incident prevailed upon me to take stock of my attitude and response to this tradition of my people.

Why am I telling you all this, my friend? To let you know what happened to me, your friend. How I worked things out to suit me, to keep my sanity.

I moved into my daughter's home two days after my grandson was born. In my musings above, you got a good idea of what took place there. You learnt how my day and night were spent. But there is something you do not know yet. It'll surprise you.

My joy went awry. Three weeks into my *omugwo* odyssey, I fainted at a board meeting, in the office. I was actually chairing the meeting.

Can I really say I didn't see it coming? I had been shuttling between my daughter's home and mine for the *omugwo*. Worse still, I had to show up at the office to do my normal job. (I assure you it is always stressful there, as there is so much to do.) Between hurrying to the office, chairing committees and running home to look after things, there was no time for relaxation.

There was no question of taking my annual leave at the time or even now. As I said, there was no moment's rest. Sleepless nights, the rush to get to work early enough, sometimes without breakfast and heavy traffic on the way to work wreaked havoc on my fragile frame. My health nose-dived, plummeted like a crashing aircraft, plunging into the dark zone of infirmity. The centre couldn't hold any longer and the body buckled under this severe stress. Did I think I was of superhuman strength? Why did I push myself to breaking point?

So my answer to your question is simple. I wasn't coping then. I simply was not able to cope. But, who said I couldn't modify *omugwo*? I acted with precision. I insisted my daughter and grandchild move into my house. My own mother didn't insist I move in with her in my childbearing days because she didn't need to. Her own mother didn't either, in her own time, because nothing called for such a dislocation in their lives. There was no need to break the form or rhythm of *omugwo*. But then neither my mother nor my grandmother worked in an office or managed a company as I do. Neither of them had to rush off at 6 o'clock, in the morning, Monday through Friday, to catch a cab or yell at a driver to make haste. None of them lived in Lagos to face its chronic, infernal traffic jam.

No, they weren't board members or heads of units or chief executives of a company. As a matter of fact, both were astute traders; they were their own bosses and decided how to use their time. They took *omugwo* within their stride.

So I subverted our tradition and survived on my own terms. *Omugwo* is made for mothers, not mothers for *omugwo*. I've learnt to 'adjust', my friend. I'm free! The arrival of my grandson does not, in the least, make me feel old. I'm bubbling with life again, after that enervating experience. Things are much better now.

Oh, well, let me not bore you with all that is on my mind. How's Inanda? I hope you're happy there? I hear it's the headquarters of a great Christian sect in South Africa. Any regrets about leaving Durban? Is this Inanda of a place a city or a rural settlement? You really haven't had time to tell me about the place, have you? Any plan to come to Lagos? Do let me know. You know you'll be welcome. Do you think it might be possible for me to visit you sometime next year? I mean after this *omugwo stuff.* I hunger for a change of scene. New desires ruffle the edges of the fabric of my heart. I long to travel again. Just a short holiday: two or three weeks.

I hope you'll find time to reply. I'll write again to let you know the progress I'm making with *omugwo.* I'm sure I'll have plenty to tell you in my next mail. Until I read from you, keep sailing and smiling.

Odiche

[First published in Adimora-Ezeigbo, Akachi and Uzoigwe, Veronica Ugbomma. (Eds). *Wings of Dawn. An Anthology of New Writing by Nigerian Women.* Lagos: The British Council. 2006, pp 113-122. Reproduced in Akachi Adimora-Ezeigbo, *Magic Breast Bags.* Ibadan: University Press Plc,

2019, pp. 115-121.]

APPENDIX II

One day, I met Ejimnaka, Obiatu's wife. It was the day she joined *alutaradi*, after her marriage. I was struck by her beauty. To behold her was to behold the glory of womanhood. Her hair was thick and stylishly plaited. The features of her comely face were clearly defined, like the outline of a well-carved mask. You can see that even the ravages of time have done little to alter those features. When I met her, she was no longer a maiden but was young. Younger than I by a few years, I thought.

Envy got into my spirit. I fought it desperately. I had never experienced such a feeling before and I was afraid. In my heart, I began to wish Ejimnaka and Obiatu ill. A strange thought had invaded my mind. I prayed to Oda and Nguma to make her barren.

I was in this state when the *nmu-oku*[1] festival arrived and my mother invited me and her other daughters to the *Ime Chi*. It was a reunion for all of us. Mother took care of us and our children throughout the days we were with her. Usually, I enjoyed the ritual of the celebration when each daughter would bend low, pick up with her mouth the small ball of *foofoo* dipped in *oha* soup which was placed on a wooden plate and then swallowed it. But on that occasion, I did it with no enthusiasm.

My mother saw my unhappiness. She took me aside that night. "Onyeka, something is wrong. You are not yourself. Something is feeding on your flesh. What is it, my daughter?" she asked with concern.

"*Nne*, nothing is wrong?" I lied. "Maybe I am tired."

"Tired, doing what?" She was not convinced. "My daughter, bare your mind to me. Tell me the truth."

I told her that the only man I ever truly desired in my life was taken away from me. She shook her head sadly. My mother could not understand me. She had advised me to do as I was told and choose a husband from the extended family and I had rejected her advice. She did not see why I should grieve.

Then she told me a story about the raven who

wanted to exchange its beautiful and shiny black feathers for the white feathers of the egret. The raven went to the river and bathed itself for a long time, but its colour would not change. No matter how hard it tried, it could not achieve its desire. Rather, its beautiful black feathers looked dull and worn after all the repeated washing.

She ended up saying that Obiatu was out of my reach. If I pined away forever, I would still not have him, for he would not leave his wife for me.

"But *Nne*," I protested, "I'm not asking that he should be my husband. I only want him as a companion."

"It is not right for you to think like that," she said, impatiently. "Obiatu is an only son. What he needs is not a companion but a wife, to bear him children who will perpetuate his name and his ancestors. You cannot be that woman. So forget him and pick up your life where you dropped it."

For many days I thought about what my mother said. The parable of the raven began to make sense. I must not hunger after what I could not have, or it would break my spirit and dry my bones.

My mother had advised me to make friends with Ejimnaka.

You know, that was exactly what I did.

One day, I sent my son to her house with a bundle of *ute* leaves and told him to say that it was a gift from a friend, and since I did not know what to do with it, she should have it.

She came to my house the following day to thank me. I returned her visit and made sure it was a time Obiatu was not at home. Our friendship grew. As time passed, the thought of Obiatu ceased to bring a sharp pain to my heart.

I taught Ejimnaka how to prepare some foods I knew Obiatu liked, and she helped me to decorate the walls of my house with *uri* and charcoal.

NOTE

1. Nmu-oku stands for Omoku (a ritual among Uga women that is now extinct).

[The passage is excerpted from my novel *The Last of the Strong Ones.* Lagos: Vista Books, 1996. Republished by Lantern Books, Literamed Publications, Lagos, 2006.]

INDEX

A

Aba Women's War, 14
Ada, 35
Adichie, 8
African Languages and Cultures, 34
African Women, 16, 40
African women writers, 8
Aguata, 13, 14, 17, 18, 36
Aguata County Council, 16
Aguluezechukwu, 17
Akachi Adimora-Ezeigbo, 16, 38, 40, 50,64
Akpo, 17
Allen, Judith van, 39
Alutaradi, 8, 11, 14, 51
Ama Ata Aidoo, 8
Amadiume, 15, 34, 39
Amesi, 17
Amma Darko, 8
Anaedobe, M. M., 39
Anambra State, 17, 18
Anthology, 30, 38, 40, 50

aspire, 7, 16

B

Basden, 11, 13, 39
Bessie Head, 8,
British, 14,
British Council, 33, 38, 40
Buchi Emecheta, 8

C

ceremony, 20
Chi, 22, 23,
Chibundu Onuzo, 8
Chika Unigwe, 8
Children of the Eagle, 18, 40
Chinua Achebe, 6
Christian, 18, 22, 50
Christiana Ukadinma Adimora, iii, 7
Christianisation, 23
Christians, 7
Church Missionary Society, 13
Colonialism, 16, 39,
consciousness, 6, 67
Content, 19, 20
coronavirus, 8

D

daughter, 20, 21, 22, 25, 27, 29, 30, 31, 35, 36, 37, 43, 45. 46, 47, 52
daughters, 8, 14, 20, 21, 26, 27, 29, 34, 35, 36, 39
decolonisation, 5
decolonised, 5
decolonising, 5
Durban, 50

E

Eastern Region of Nigeria, 7
Ejimnaka, 28, 29, 51, 53, 54
Ekwulobia, 7, 17
excerpted, 54
Ezeigbo, T. Akachi, 39, 64
Ezenwaka, Titus N., 39

F

female children, 21, 31, 35
female novelists, 8
Festival of Ideas, 5
first daughter, 21, 35
Flora Nwapa, 8
foofoo, 21, 52
form, 19, 20, 23, 33, 49
forms, 9,

G

gender, 7, 10, 14,
Gender Issues in Nigeria, 15, 39,
Gender-based violence, 9
global, 5, 6, 23
globalisation, 23
grand, 30, 44, 45
GRAND EXPERIENCE, 30, 38, 41 ,
grandmother, 30, 31, 38, 42, 45, 47, 49,
grandmothers, 13,

H

House of Symbols, 18, 40
human rights, 9

I

Idemmiri, 36
Ifeoma Okoye, 8
Ifi Amadiume, 34, 39
Igbo, 8, 14, 15, 16, 17, 19, 26, 32, 34, 35,
Igbo families, 32, 34, 36
Igbo Female, 34, 39
Igbo Society, 19, 34, 39
Igbo women, 11, 13, 14, 15, 16, 19, 21, 23, 32, 35, 39,
Igboland, 10, 13, 14, 16, 18, 23, 26, 36,
Ime Chi, 10, 11, 18, 19, 20, 22, 26, 27, 32, 38, 51,

Inanda, 50
Institutions, 5, 10, 11, 19, 20, 32, 38, 39, 7, 35
Isigwu, 36
Isuofia, 17

J

Jesus Christ, 33

K

Kaine Agary, 8
knowledge, 3, 4, 5, 7, 11, 38

L

leadership, 9, 10, 11, 15, 16, 17, 18, 19, 21, 26, 27, 29, 32, 33
Leith-Ross, 16, 40
Lola Shoneyin, 8

M

Male Daughters, Female Husbands, 34, 39
modernity, 23
modify, 48
mother, 7, 17, 20, 21, 22, 23, 24, 26, 27, 28, 29, 30, 31, 36, 41, 43, 44, 45, 46, 47, 49, 51, 52, 53,
mothers, 18, 23, 24, 26, 27, 34, 49,

N

Nanka, 17
Nawal El Saadawi, 6
Ndi Igbo, 11, 13, 16, 22, 23, 26, 27
Nigerian, 8, 9, 34, 38, 40, 50
Nina Emma Mba, 34, 40
Nkpologwu, 17
Nmu-oku, 51, 54
NoViolet Bulawayo, 8

O

Obiabaka, Amamchukwu., 24, 40
Obiatu, 26, 25, 45, 47, 48, 49
Odoala, 22, 35, 36
oha, 22, 52
Oko, 17
Omoku, 10, 11, 18, 19, 20, 22, 26, 27, 28, 29, 32, 38, 54
Omugwo, 10, 11, 18, 19, 20, 23, 24, 25, 26, 29, 30, 31, 32, 34, 36, 40, 46, 47, 48, 49, 50,
Onyeka, 52
Onyekozuru, 27, 28, 29,

P

patriarchy, 14, 26
political, 11, 14, 15, 16, 26, 34, 39, 40
politics, 17

Port Harcourt, 7
Promise Ogochukwu, 8
protagonist, 30

R

raven, 28, 29, 52
Rebecca Njau, 8
reclaim, 6
research, 8, 9, 18, 32, 36,
ritual, 19, 20, 21, 22, 25, 27, 30, 35, 36, 43, 52, 54,
rituals, 18, 19, 22, 38

S

scholarship, 5
School of Oriental and African Studies, 5
Sefi Atta, 8
Servant leader, 37
servant leaders, 32
service, 32, 33
sex, 14
sit, 16,
Sitting on a Man, 16, 39
snails, 21
social systems, 14

T

Traditional Women's Institutions, 34, 39

U

Uga, 7, 14, 17, 18, 19, 21, 22, 35, 36, 39, 40, 54
Ukwu, 17
Umuada, 8, 11, 14, 15
Umuchu, 17
Umuga, 18, 29
une oji, 22
ungrandmotherly, 42
University of London, 5
Unoma Azuah, 8
utara ede, 22

V

Veronica Ugbomma Uzoigwe, 38, 40, 50
Virtual SOAS, 5

W

wife, 17, 22, 28, 51, 53
woman, 7, 20, 22, 23, 24, 25, 27, 30, 31, 32, 35, 36, 37, 46, 53
women, 7, 8, 9, 10, 11, 13, 14, 15, 16, 17, 18, 22, 23, 24, 25, 26, 32, 34, 35, 36, 38, 40, 50,
women's institutions, 18,

Women Mobilized, 34, 40
Women's Political Activity, 34, 40
WRITA, 38, 40

Y

Yoruba, 26
youths, 16
Yvonne Vera, 8

Z

Zaynab Alkali, 8
Zimela, 41

LIST OF PUBLICATIONS

Also by T. Akachi Ezeigbo
(Writing under the Pen Name Akachi Adimora-Ezeigbo)

NOVELS

- *The Last of the Strong Ones*
- *House of Symbols*
- *Children of the Eagle*
- *Trafficked*
- *Roses and Bullets*

SHORT STORY COLLECTIONS

- *Rhythms of Life, Stories of Modern Nigeria*
- *Rituals and Departures*
- *Echoes in the Mind*
- *Fractures and Fragments*
- *Magic Breast Bags*

POEMS

- *Heart Songs*
- *Waiting for Dawn*
- *Cloud and Other Poems for Children*
- *The Eagle and Other Poems for Secondary Schools*
- *Dancing Masks*
- *Singing in the Rain and Other Poems for Children*
- *Mixed Legacies*

PLAYS

- *Hands that Crush Stone*
- *Barmaid and the Witches of Izunga*

CHILDREN'S FICTION

- *The Buried Treasure*
- *The Prize*
- *Alani the Troublemaker and other Stories*
- *Asa and the Little Stream*
- *Whisker the Brave Cat*
- *Red One and the Wizard of Mula*
- *Sunshine the Miracle Child*
- *Snake Child and Star Baby*
- *Ezezemale and the Tree Spirits*

- *Adventures of Anum the Tortoise*
- *My Cousin Sammy*
- *Fire from the Holy Mountain*
- *Ako the Storyteller*
- *Zoba and his Gang*
- *The Slave Girl,*
- *The Dwarf's Story*
- *The Return of the Thief*
- *The Boy and the Dog*
- *Mina the Shy Girl*
- *Toki Learns the Hard Way*
- *Seyi's Strong Voice*
- *Kidnapped at Noon*
- *Ona and the Dwarf* (with Odinaka Azubuike)

NON-FICTION

- *Fact and Fiction in the Literature of the Nigerian Civil War*
- *Gender Issues in Nigeria: A Feminine Perspective*
- *A Companion to the Novel*
- *Artistic Creativity: Literature in the Service of Society*
- *Snail-Sense Feminism: Building on an Indigenous Model*

- *The Literatures of War* (edited with Liz Gunner)
- *Wings of Dawn* (edited with Ronnie Uzoigwe)
- *Literature, Language and National Consciousness: A Festschrift in Honour of Theo Vincent* (edited with Karen King-Aribisala)
- *Things Fall Apart @ 50* (edited with Adetokunbo Pearse)

Printed in Great Britain
by Amazon

66212084R00041